Know the World!

David Green

Tarquin Publications

√F⌐

What do you know?

There are hundreds of names in this book and nobody can be expected to know them all.....
Or can they?

Test your knowledge of the world's geography by putting places on the map! Find an atlas and get your family and friends to help.....

The idea is simple: each of the 30 outline maps is accompanied by a list of countries, cities, rivers, mountains and seas. Your job is to put the names on the maps in the right place. See how far you can get before you need to consult the atlas.....

You will find there is no better way of memorising maps than by this do-it-yourself method.

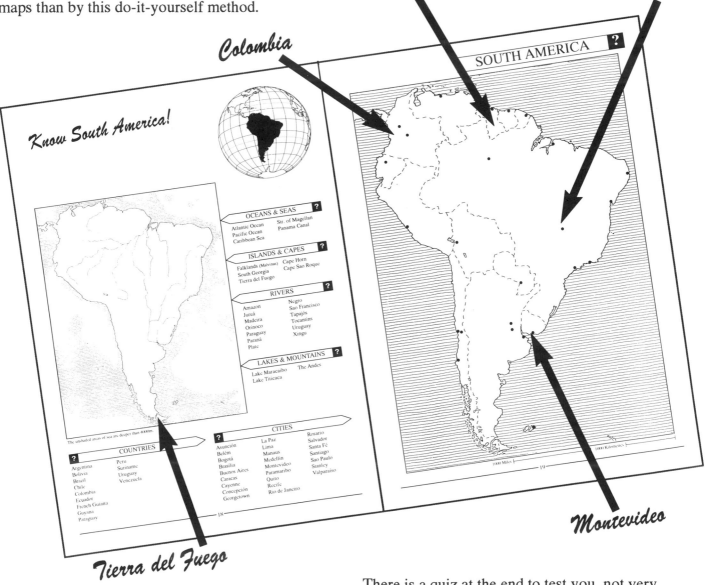

Guyana

Brasilia

Colombia

Know South America!

SOUTH AMERICA

OCEANS & SEAS
Atlantic Ocean   Str. of Magellan
Pacific Ocean   Panama Canal
Caribbean Sea

ISLANDS & CAPES
Falklands (Malvinas)   Cape Horn
South Georgia   Cape Sao Roque
Tierra del Fuego

RIVERS
Amazon   Negro
Juruá   San Francisco
Madeira   Tapajós
Orinoco   Tocantins
Paraguay   Uruguay
Paraná   Xingu
Plate

LAKES & MOUNTAINS
Lake Maracaibo   The Andes
Lake Titicaca

COUNTRIES
Argentina   Peru
Bolivia   Suriname
Brazil   Uruguay
Chile   Venezuela
Colombia
Ecuador
French Guiana
Guyana
Paraguay

CITIES
Asunción   La Paz   Rosario
Belém   Lima   Salvador
Bogotá   Manaus   Santa Fé
Brasilia   Medellín   Santiago
Buenos Aires Montevideo Sao Paulo
Caracas   Paramaribo   Stanley
Cayenne   Quito   Valparaíso
Concepción Recife
Georgetown Rio de Janeiro

The unshaded areas of sea are deeper than 4000m.

1000 Miles   1000 Kilometres

Tierra del Fuego

Montevideo

There is a quiz at the end to test you, not very seriously, on your new-found geographical skills.....

THE WORLD ?

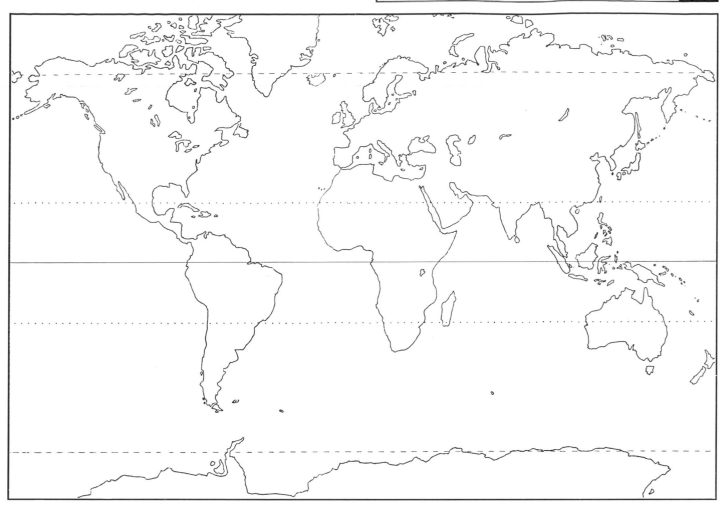

? CONTINENTS

Africa
Antarctica
Asia
Australasia
Europe
North America
South America

? OCEANS

Arctic
Atlantic
Indian
Pacific
Southern

? LINES OF LATITUDE

Arctic Circle
Antarctic Circle
Equator
Tropic of Cancer
Tropic of Capricorn

? ISLANDS

Australia
Borneo
Great Britain
Greenland
Iceland
Ireland
Madagascar
New Guinea
New Zealand
Japan

? MOUNTAINS

Alps
Andes
Himalayas
Rockies
Urals

? DESERTS

Arabian
Arizona
Atacama
Gobi
Great Australian
Kalahari
Sahara

Know Europe!

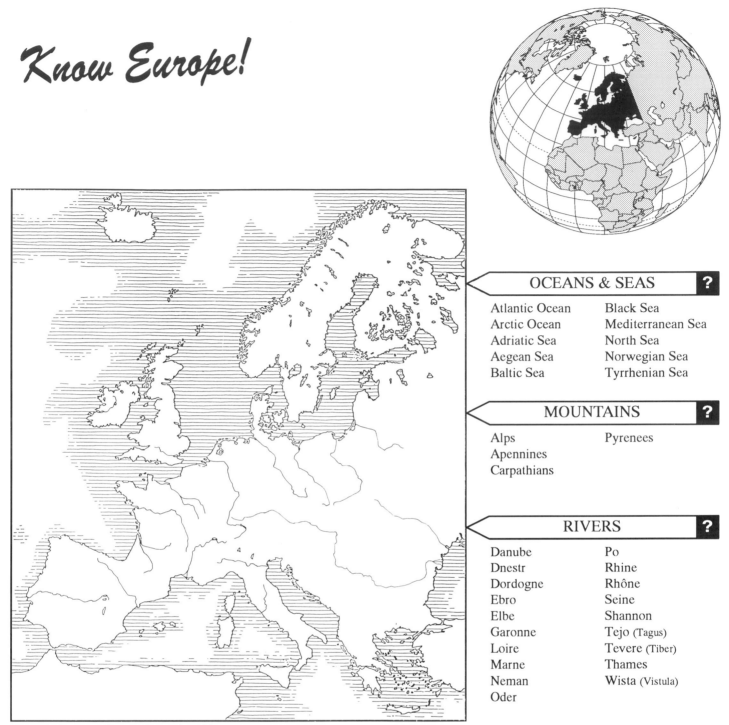

The unshaded areas of sea are deeper than 200m.

OCEANS & SEAS ?

Atlantic Ocean	Black Sea
Arctic Ocean	Mediterranean Sea
Adriatic Sea	North Sea
Aegean Sea	Norwegian Sea
Baltic Sea	Tyrrhenian Sea

MOUNTAINS ?

Alps	Pyrenees
Apennines	
Carpathians	

RIVERS ?

Danube	Po
Dnestr	Rhine
Dordogne	Rhône
Ebro	Seine
Elbe	Shannon
Garonne	Tejo (Tagus)
Loire	Tevere (Tiber)
Marne	Thames
Neman	Wista (Vistula)
Oder	

? COUNTRIES

Albania	Italy	Switzerland
Andorra	Latvia	Turkey
Austria	Lithuania	Ukraine
Belgium	Luxembourg	United Kingdom
Belorussia	Moldavia	(Yugoslavia) now
Bulgaria	Netherlands	Bosnia-Hertzegovina
Czech Republic	Norway	Croatia
Denmark	Poland	Kosovo
Estonia	Portugal	Macedonia
Finland	Rep. of Ireland	Montenegro
France	Romania	Serbia
Germany	Russian Federation	Slovenia
Greece	Slovakia	
Hungary	Spain	
Iceland	Sweden	

? CITIES

Amsterdam	Lisboa (Lisbon)	Tiranë (Tirana)
Athínai (Athens)	London	Vilnius
Beograd (Belgrade)	Madrid	Warszawa (Warsaw)
Berlin	Monte-Carlo	Wien (Vienna)
Bern (Berne)	Minsk	Zagreb
Bratislava	Oslo	
Bruxelles (Brussels)	Paris	
Bucuresti (Bucharest)	Praha (Prague)	
Budapest	Sofiya (Sofia)	
Dublin	Reykjavik	
Helsinki	Riga	
Kaliningrad	Roma (Rome)	
Kiyev (Kiev)	Sarajevo	
Kishinev	Stockholm	
København (Copenhagen)	Tallinn	

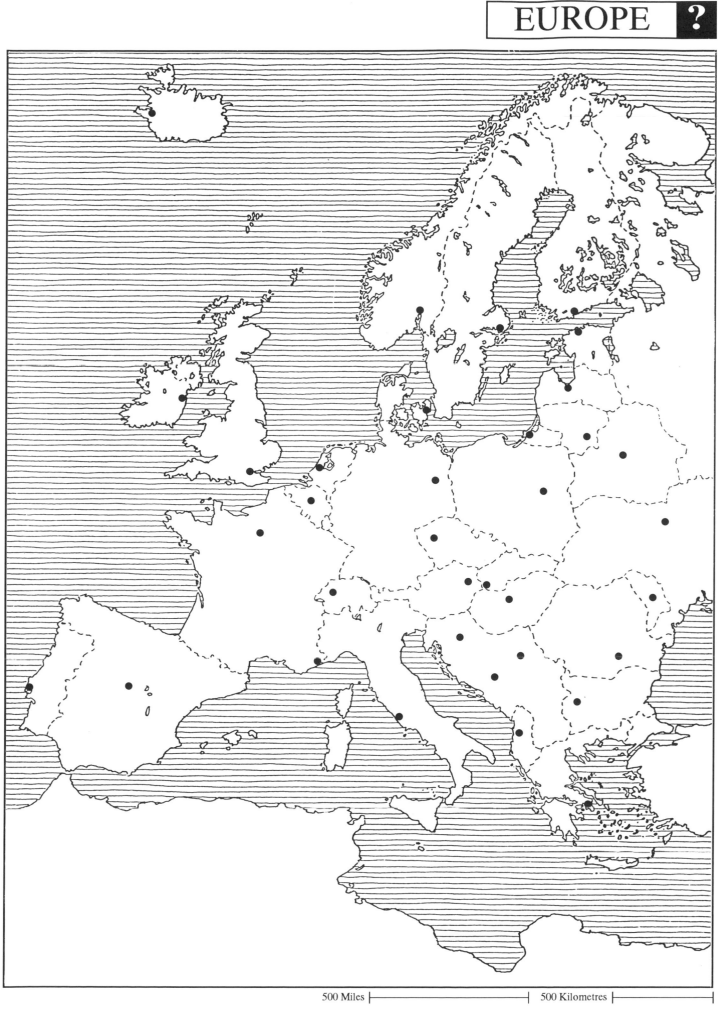

500 Miles

500 Kilometres

The unshaded areas of sea are deeper than 200m.

OCEANS & SEAS ?

Atlantic Ocean	The Minches
Bristol Channel	Moray Firth
English Channel	North Sea
Firth of Clyde	Pentland Firth
Firth of Forth	Solway Firth
Irish Sea	The Wash

ISLANDS

Anglesey	Mull
Isle of Man	Outer Hebrides
Isle of Wight	Skye

RIVERS ?

Clyde	Tay
Great Ouse	Tees
Little Ouse	Thames
Yorkshire Ouse	Trent
Severn	Tyne
Shannon	

MOUNTAINS & HILLS

Ben Nevis	Cheviot Hills
Mount Snowdon	Grampian Mountains
Scafell Pike	Pennine Hills

? COUNTIES & REGIONS

ENGLAND

1. Avon
2. Bedfordshire
3. Berkshire
4. Buckinghamshire
5. Cambridgeshire
6. Cheshire
7. Cleveland
8. Cornwall
9. Cumbria
10. Derbyshire
11. Devon
12. Dorset
13. Durham
14. Essex
15. Gloucestershire
16. Greater London
17. Greater Manchester
18. Hampshire
19. Hereford & Worcester
20. Hertfordshire
21. Humberside
22. Isle of Wight
23. Kent
24. Lancashire
25. Leicestershire
26. Lincolnshire
27. Merseyside
28. Norfolk
29. Northamptonshire
30. Northumberland
31. Nottinghamshire
32. Oxfordshire
33. Shropshire
34. Somerset
35. Staffordshire
36. Suffolk
37. Surrey
38. East Sussex
39. West Sussex
40. Tyne & Wear
41. Warwickshire
42. West Midlands
43. Wiltshire
44. North Yorkshire
45. West Yorkshire
46. South Yorkshire

WALES

1. Clwyd
2. Dyfed
3. Mid Glamorgan
4. South Glamorgan
5. West Glamorgan
6. Gwent
7. Gwynedd
8. Powys

SCOTLAND

1. Borders
2. Central
3. Dumfries & Galloway
4. Fife
5. Grampian
6. Highland
7. Lothian
8. Orkney
9. Shetland
10. Strathclyde
11. Tayside
12. Western Isles

N.IRELAND

1. Antrim
2. Armagh
3. Down
4. Fermanagh
5. Londonderry
6. Tyrone

? CITIES & TOWNS

Aberdeen	Lincoln
Aberystwyth	Liverpool
Bangor	London
Belfast	Londonderry
Birmingham	Manchester
Bristol	Newcastle
Cambridge	Nottingham
Cardiff	Norwich
Dover	Oxford
Dundee	Plymouth
Durham	Sheffield
Edinburgh	Southampton
Exeter	Swansea
Glasgow	Worcester
Gloucester	York
Hull	
Inverness	
Ipswich	
Leeds	
Leicester	

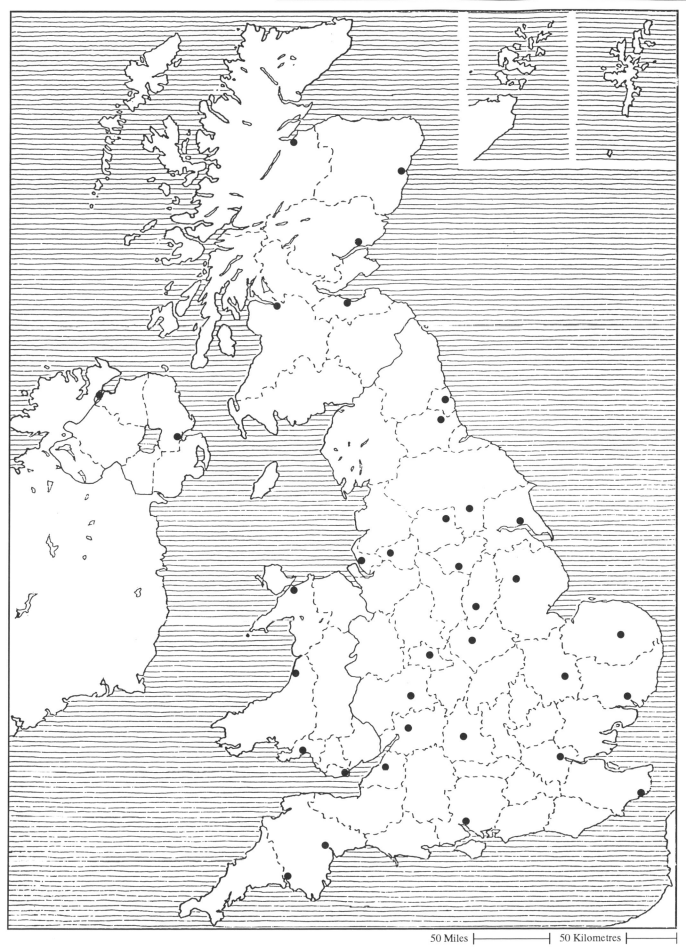

50 Miles | 50 Kilometres |

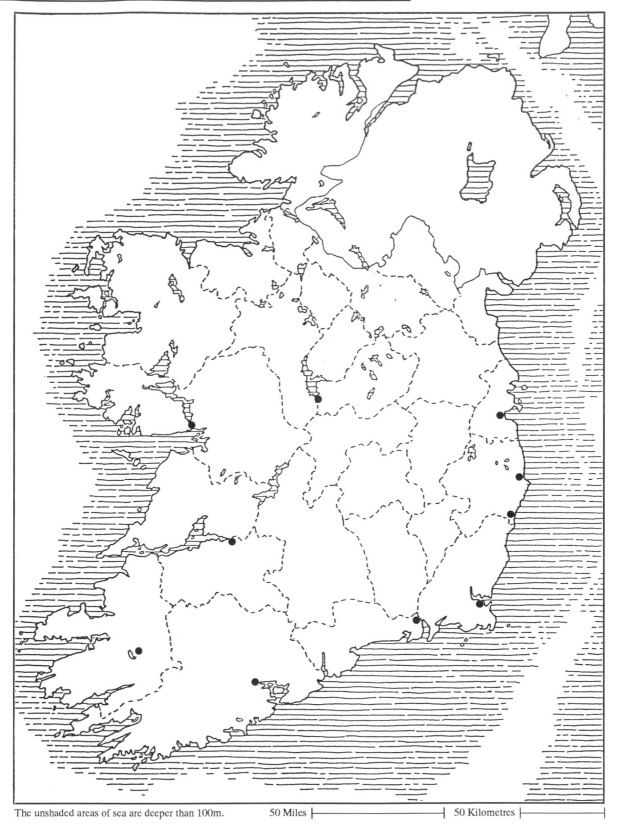

The unshaded areas of sea are deeper than 100m.　　50 Miles ├────────┤　　50 Kilometres ├────────┤

? COUNTIES			
Carlow	Kerry	Louth	Tipperary
Cavan	Kildare	Mayo	Waterford
Clare	Kilkenny	Meath	Westmeath
Cork	Laois	Monaghan	Wexford
Donegal	Leitrim	Offaly	Wicklow
Dublin	Limerick	Roscommon	
Galway	Longford	Sligo	

? CITIES & TOWNS	
Arklow	Killarney
Athlone	Limerick
Cork	Waterford
Dublin	Wexford
Galway	Wicklow

THE MEDITERRANEAN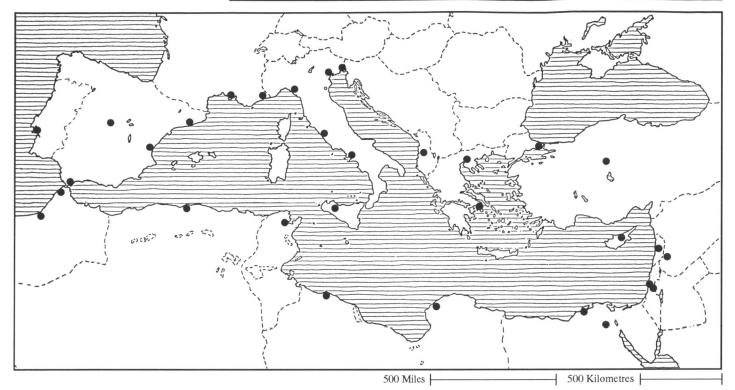

500 Miles | | 500 Kilometres | |

? SEAS & ISLANDS

Atlantic Ocean	Corse (Corsica)
Aegean Sea	Kérkira (Corfu)
Black Sea	Kríti (Crete)
Ionian Sea	Cyprus
Tyrrhenian Sea	Ibiza
Sea of Azov	Mallorca (Majorca)
Sea of Marmara	Menorca
Str. of Gibraltar	Sardegna (Sardinia)
Str. of Messina	Sicilia (Sicily)
Str. of Otranto	
Suez Canal	

? COUNTRIES

Albania	Romania
Algeria	Saudi Arabia
Austria	Spain
Bulgaria	Switzerland
Egypt	Syria
France	Tunisia
Greece	Turkey
Hungary	Ukraine
Israel	(Yugoslavia) now
Italy	Bosnia-Hertzegovina
Jordan	Croatia
Lebanon	Kosovo
Libya	Macedonia
Moldavia	Montenegro
Morocco	Serbia
Portugal	Slovenia

? CITIES

Alexandria	Napoli (Naples)
Alger (Algiers)	Nice
Ankara	Nicosia
Athínai (Athens)	Palermo
Barcelona	Rabat
Benghazi	Roma (Rome)
Beyrouth (Beirut)	Thessaloniki (Salonica)
Cairo	Tanger (Tangiers)
Dimashq (Damascus)	Tarabulus (Tripoli)
Genova (Genoa)	Tel Aviv
Gibraltar	Tiranë (Tirana)
Istanbul	Trieste
Jerusalem	Tunis
Lisboa (Lisbon)	Valencia
Madrid	Venezia (Venice)
Marseille	

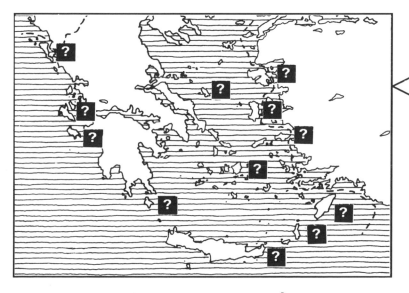

GREEK ISLANDS ?

Cephalonia	Lesbos
Chios	Naxos
Corfu	Rhodes
Crete	Samos
Karpathos	Skiros
Kithira	Zante

Know Africa!

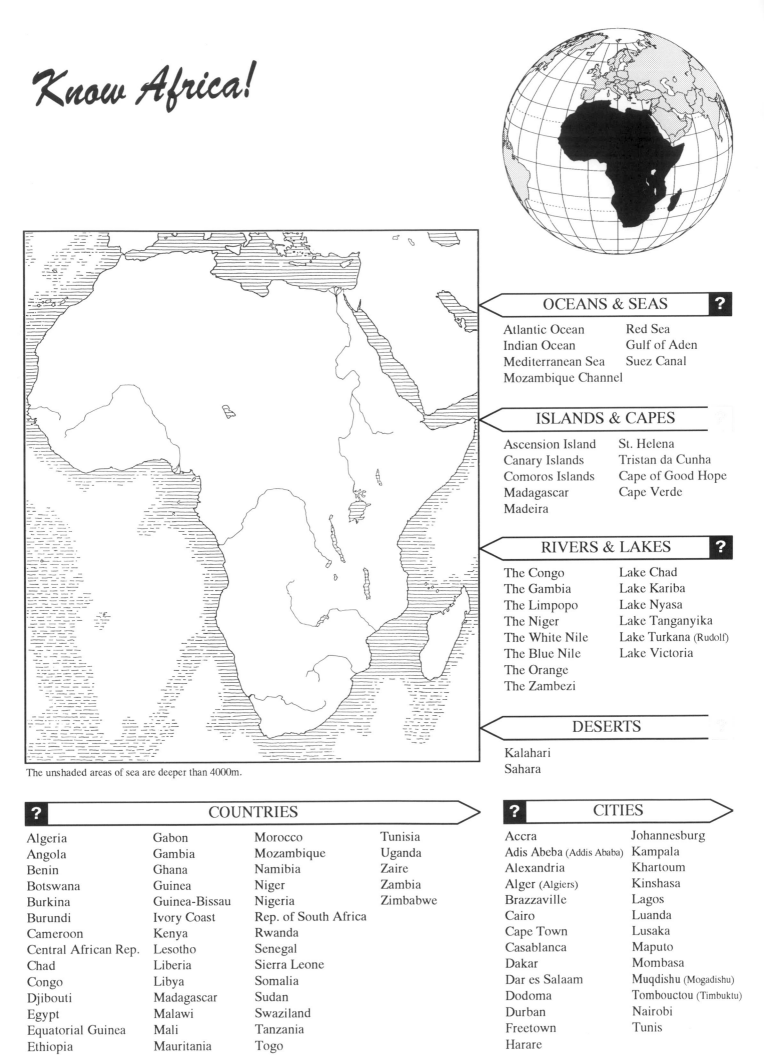

OCEANS & SEAS   ?

Atlantic Ocean	Red Sea
Indian Ocean	Gulf of Aden
Mediterranean Sea	Suez Canal
Mozambique Channel	

ISLANDS & CAPES

Ascension Island	St. Helena
Canary Islands	Tristan da Cunha
Comoros Islands	Cape of Good Hope
Madagascar	Cape Verde
Madeira	

RIVERS & LAKES   ?

The Congo	Lake Chad
The Gambia	Lake Kariba
The Limpopo	Lake Nyasa
The Niger	Lake Tanganyika
The White Nile	Lake Turkana (Rudolf)
The Blue Nile	Lake Victoria
The Orange	
The Zambezi	

DESERTS

Kalahari
Sahara

?   COUNTRIES

Algeria	Gabon	Morocco	Tunisia
Angola	Gambia	Mozambique	Uganda
Benin	Ghana	Namibia	Zaire
Botswana	Guinea	Niger	Zambia
Burkina	Guinea-Bissau	Nigeria	Zimbabwe
Burundi	Ivory Coast	Rep. of South Africa	
Cameroon	Kenya	Rwanda	
Central African Rep.	Lesotho	Senegal	
Chad	Liberia	Sierra Leone	
Congo	Libya	Somalia	
Djibouti	Madagascar	Sudan	
Egypt	Malawi	Swaziland	
Equatorial Guinea	Mali	Tanzania	
Ethiopia	Mauritania	Togo	

?   CITIES

Accra	Johannesburg
Adis Abeba (Addis Ababa)	Kampala
Alexandria	Khartoum
Alger (Algiers)	Kinshasa
Brazzaville	Lagos
Cairo	Luanda
Cape Town	Lusaka
Casablanca	Maputo
Dakar	Mombasa
Dar es Salaam	Muqdishu (Mogadishu)
Dodoma	Tombouctou (Timbuktu)
Durban	Nairobi
Freetown	Tunis
Harare	

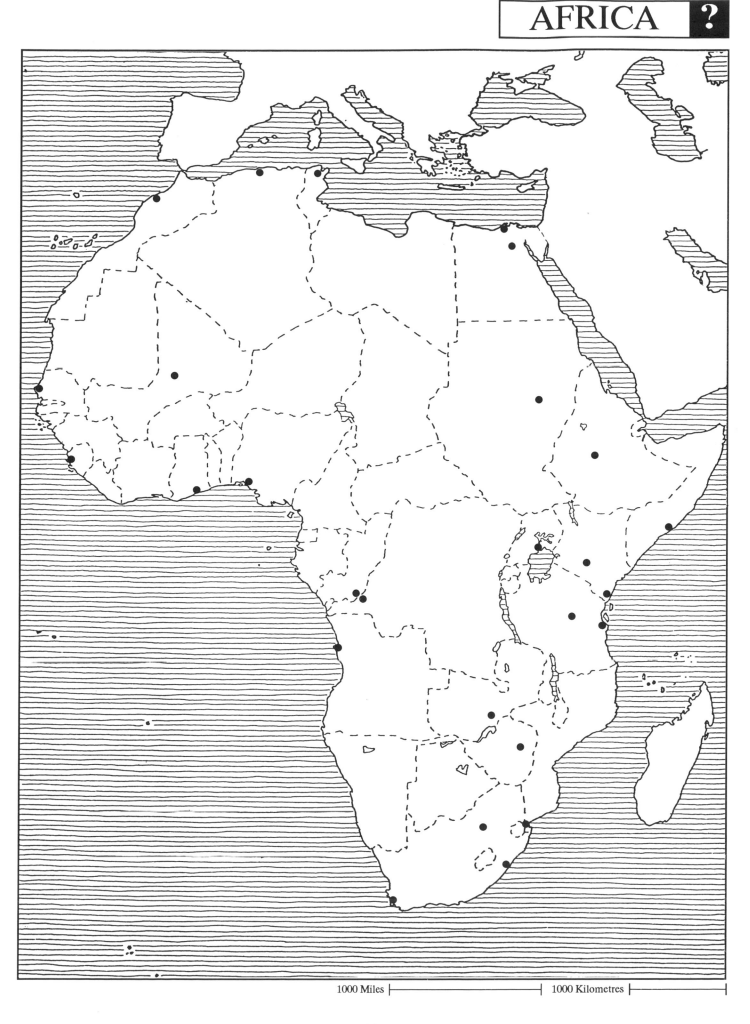

1000 Miles

1000 Kilometres

Know North America!

SEAS & ISLANDS

Arctic Ocean	Bering Str.
Atlantic Ocean	Davis Str.
Pacific Ocean	Baffin Island
Bering Sea	Bahamas
Caribbean Sea	Cuba
Gulf of California	Greenland
Gulf of Honduras	Hispaniola
Gulf of Mexico	Jamaica
Gulf of Panama	Kodiak Island
Baffin Bay	Newfoundland
Bay of Campeche	Puerto Rico
Hudson Bay	Vancouver Island
Panama Canal	Victoria Island

LAKES & RIVERS

Lake Athabaska	The Colorado
Lake Erie	The Columbia
Great Bear Lake	The Mackenzie
Great Salt Lake	The Mississippi
Great Slave Lake	The Missouri
Lake Huron	The Ohio
Lake Michigan	The Rio Grande
Lake Nicaragua	The Saskatchewan
Lake Ontario	The St. Lawrence
Lake Superior	The Yukon
Lake Winnipeg	

MOUNTAINS ?

Alaska Range	Sierra Madre
Appalachians	Sierra Nevada
Rockies	

The unshaded areas of sea are sometimes impassable due to ice.

? COUNTRIES

Belize	Haiti
Canada	Honduras
El Salvador	Jamaica
Costa Rica	Mexico
Cuba	Nicaragua
Dominican Rep.	Panama
Greenland	Puerto Rico
Guatemala	U.S.A.

? CITIES

Belmopan	Guatemala City	New Orleans	San Salvador
Boston	Habana (Havana)	New York	Santo Dominigo
Calgary	Juneau	Monterrey	Seattle
Chicago	Kingston	Ottawa	Toronto
Detroit	Los Angeles	Port au Prince	Vancouver
Fairbanks	Managua	Québec	Washington
Gödthab	Mexico City	San Francisco	Winnipeg
Guadalajara	Montreal (Montréal)	San José	

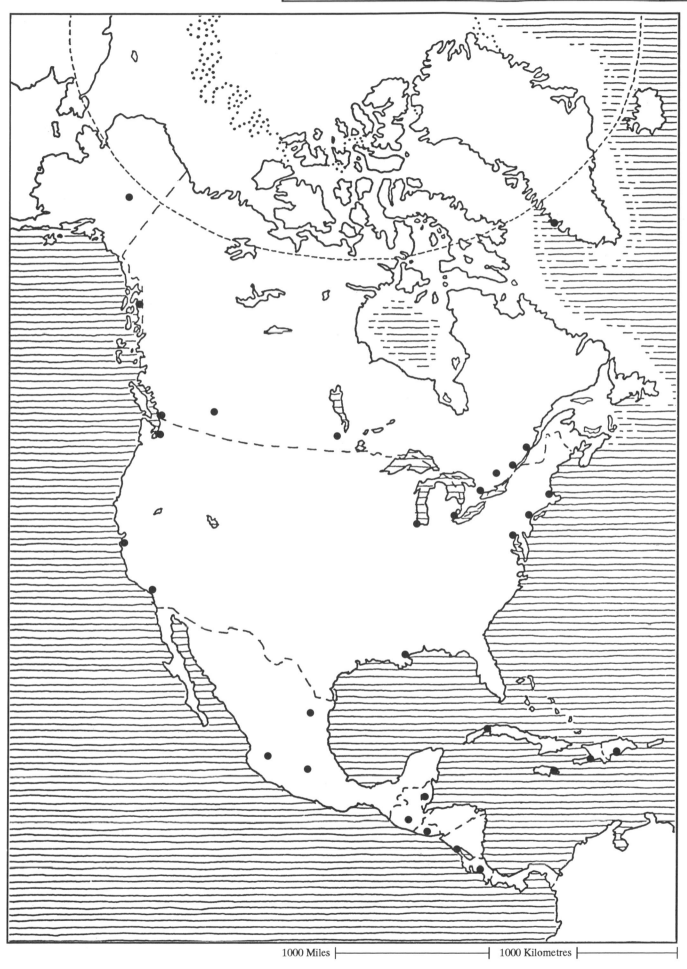

1000 Miles |⊢——————————⊣| 1000 Kilometres |⊢——————————⊣|

? UNITED STATES OF AMERICA

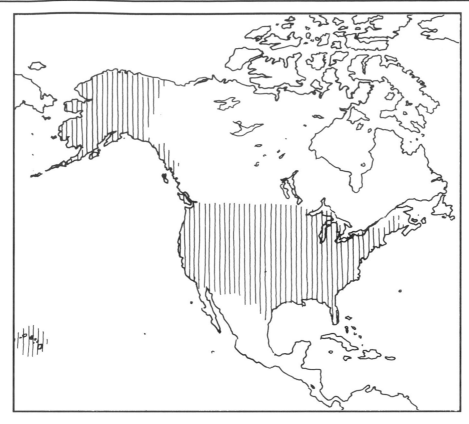

? CITIES

Albuquerque	Detroit	Nashville
Anchorage	Fairbanks	New Orleans
Atlanta	Houston	New York
Baltimore	Indianapolis	Philadelphia
Boston	Juneau	Pittsburgh
Chicago	Los Angeles	San Francisco
Cincinnati	Memphis	Salt Lake City
Cleveland	Miami	Seattle
Dallas	Milwaukee	Washington D.C.
Denver	Minneapolis	

? STATES (Zip Codes)

Alabama (AL)	Louisiana (LA)	Ohio (OH)
Alaska (AK)	Maine (ME)	Oklahoma (OK)
Arizona (AZ)	Maryland (MD)	Oregon (OR)
Arkansas (AR)	Massachusetts (MA)	Pennsylvania (PA)
California (CA)	Michigan (MI)	Rhode Island (RI)
Colorado (CO)	Minnesota (MN)	South Carolina (SC)
Connecticut (CT)	Mississippi (MS)	South Dakota (SD)
Delaware (DE)	Missouri (MO)	Tennessee (TN)
Florida (FL)	Montana (MT)	Texas (TX)
Georgia (GA)	Nebraska (NE)	Utah (UT)
Hawaii (HI) (see below)	Nevada (NV)	Vermont (VT)
Idaho (ID)	New Hampshire (NH)	Virginia (VA)
Illinois (IL)	New Jersey (NJ)	Washington (WA)
Indiana (IN)	New Mexico (NM)	West Virginia (WV)
Iowa (IA)	New York (NY)	Wisconsin (WI)
Kansas (KS)	North Carolina (NC)	Wyoming (WY)
Kentucky (KY)	North Dakota (ND)	

HAWAIIAN ISLANDS

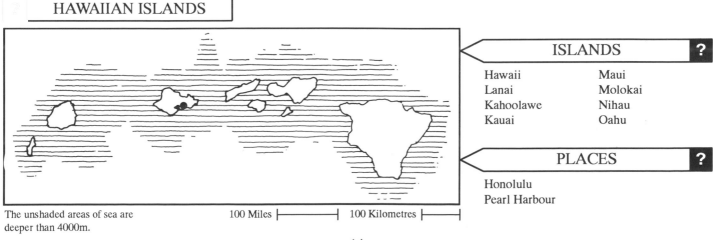

The unshaded areas of sea are deeper than 4000m.

100 Miles ├────┤   100 Kilometres ├────┤

? ISLANDS

Hawaii	Maui
Lanai	Molokai
Kahoolawe	Nihau
Kauai	Oahu

? PLACES

Honolulu
Pearl Harbour

UNITED STATES OF AMERICA

500 Miles ├─────────────────┤ 500 Kilometres ├─────────────────┤

ALASKA

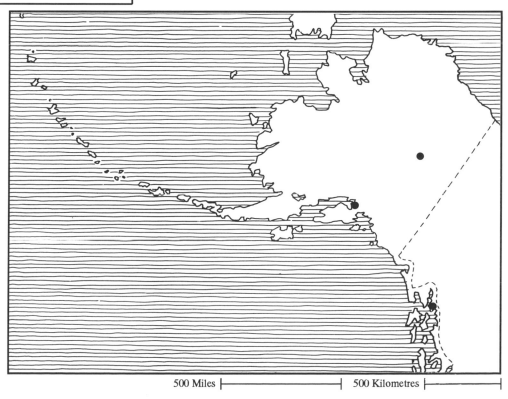

500 Miles ├─────────────────┤ 500 Kilometres ├─────────────────┤

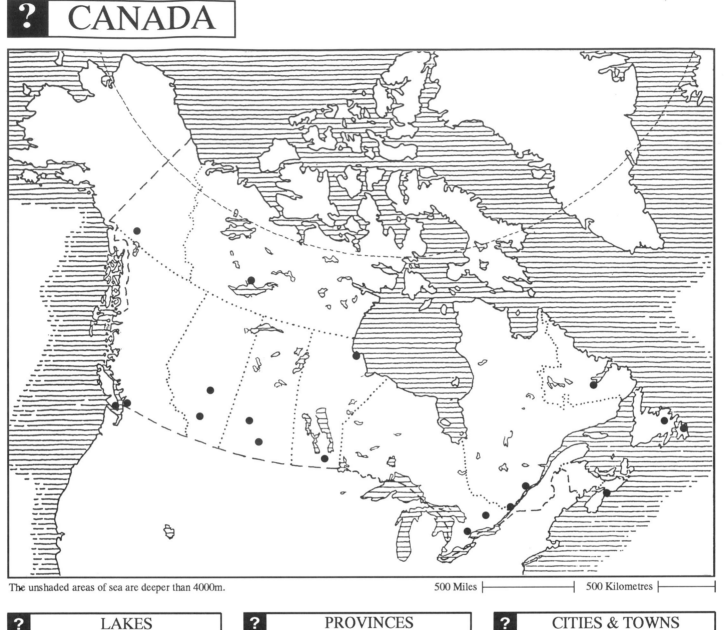

? CANADA

The unshaded areas of sea are deeper than 4000m.

500 Miles ├─────┤   500 Kilometres ├─────┤

? LAKES	
The Great Lakes	Lake Winnipegosis
Great Bear Lake	Lake of the Woods
Great Slave Lake	
Reindeer Lake	
Lake Athabaska	
Lake Winnipeg	
Lake Manitoba	

? PROVINCES	
Alberta	North West Territories
British Columbia	Nova Scotia
Labrador	Ontario
Manitoba	Prince Edward Island
New Brunswick	Québec
Newfoundland	Saskatchewan
	Yukon Territory

? CITIES & TOWNS	
Calgary	Regina
Churchill	Saskatoon
Edmonton	St. John's
Gander	Toronto
Goose Bay	Victoria
Halifax	Vancouver
Montreal (Montréal)	Whitehorse
Ottawa	Winnipeg
Québec City	Yellowknife

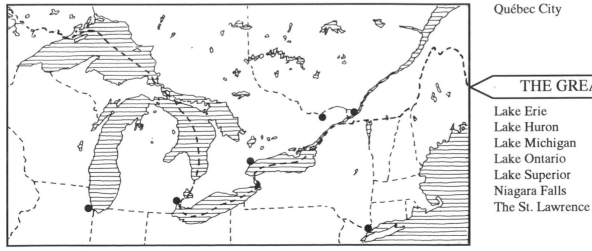

THE GREAT LAKES ?

Lake Erie	Chicago
Lake Huron	Detroit
Lake Michigan	Montreal (Montréal)
Lake Ontario	New York
Lake Superior	Ottawa
Niagara Falls	Toronto
The St. Lawrence	

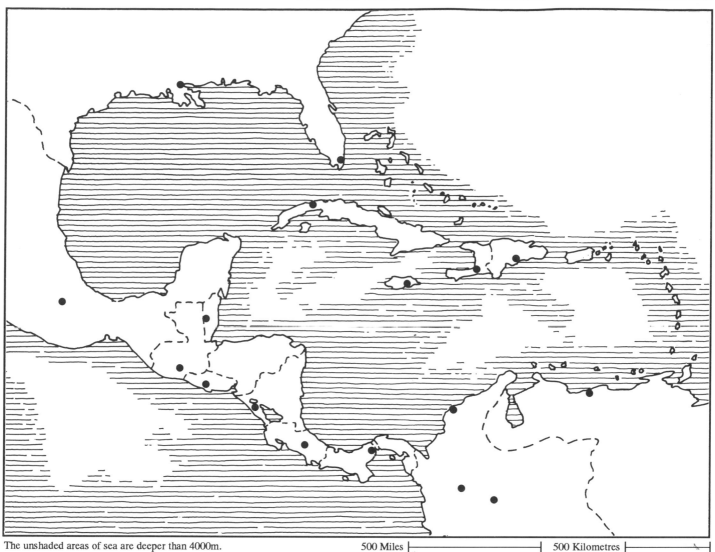

The unshaded areas of sea are deeper than 4000m.

500 Miles ├──────────┤   500 Kilometres ├──────────┤

?   OCEANS & SEAS

Atlantic Ocean	Bay of Campeche
Pacific Ocean	Str. of Florida
Caribbean Sea	Windward Passage
Gulf of Honduras	Yucatan Channel
Gulf of Mexico	Panama Canal
Gulf of Panama	

?   COUNTRIES

Belize	Guatemala	Panama
Colombia	Haiti	Puerto Rico
Costa Rica	Honduras	U.S.A.
Cuba	Jamaica	Venezuela
Dominican Rep.	Mexico	
El Salvador	Nicaragua	

?   ISLANDS

Greater Antilles
Lesser Antilles
Netherland Antilles
Bahamas
Leeward Islands
Tobago
Trinidad
Windward Islands

?   CITIES & TOWNS

Barranquilla	Mexico City
Belmopan	Miami
Bogotá	New Orleans
Caracas	Panama City
Guatemala City	Port au Prince
Habana (Havana)	San José
Kingston	San Salvador
Managua	Santo Dominigo
Medellin	

Know South America!

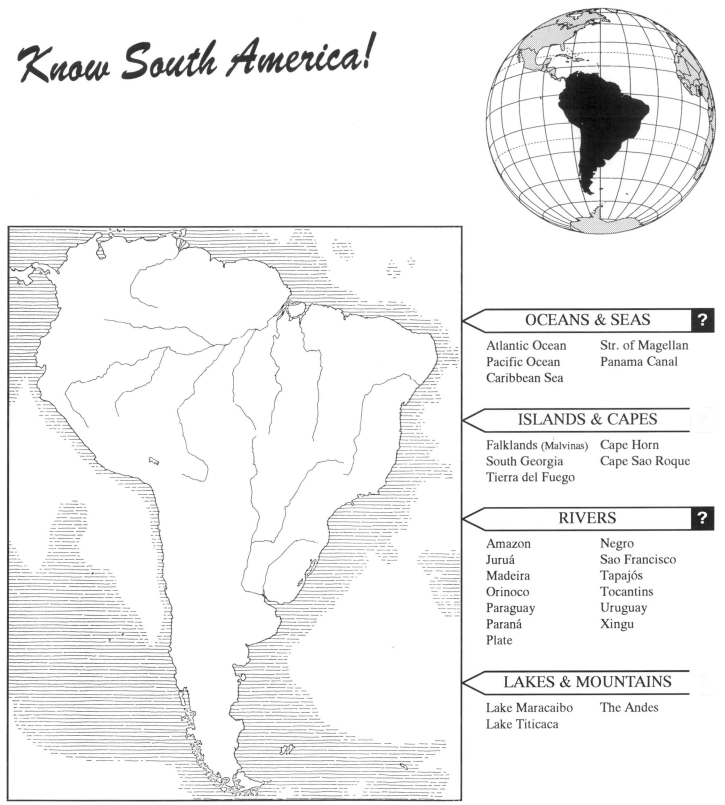

The unshaded areas of sea are deeper than 4000m.

OCEANS & SEAS ?

Atlantic Ocean	Str. of Magellan
Pacific Ocean	Panama Canal
Caribbean Sea	

ISLANDS & CAPES

Falklands (Malvinas)	Cape Horn
South Georgia	Cape Sao Roque
Tierra del Fuego	

RIVERS ?

Amazon	Negro
Juruá	Sao Francisco
Madeira	Tapajós
Orinoco	Tocantins
Paraguay	Uruguay
Paraná	Xingu
Plate	

LAKES & MOUNTAINS

Lake Maracaibo	The Andes
Lake Titicaca	

? COUNTRIES

Argentina	Peru
Bolivia	Suriname
Brazil	Uruguay
Chile	Venezuela
Colombia	
Ecuador	
French Guiana	
Guyana	
Paraguay	

? CITIES

Asunción	La Paz	Rosario
Belém	Lima	Salvador
Bogotá	Manaus	Santa Fé
Brasília	Medellin	Santiago
Buenos Aires	Montevideo	Sao Paulo
Caracas	Paramaribo	Stanley
Cayenne	Quito	Valparaíso
Concepción	Recife	
Georgetown	Rio de Janeiro	

1000 Miles ⊢   ⊢ 1000 Kilometres ⊢

Know Australasia!

? THE WESTERN PACIFIC

? LARGE ISLANDS

Australia
Borneo
Japan
Java
Hainan
New Guinea
New Zealand
Philippines
Sulawesi (Celebes)
Sumatra
Taiwan
Tasmania

? OCEANS & SEAS

Indian Ocean
Pacific Ocean
Arafura Sea
Banda Sea
East China Sea
South China Sea
Coral Sea
Sea of Okhotsk
Tasman Sea
Timor Sea
Yellow Sea

? PENINSULAS

Kamchatka
Korean
Malay

? CITIES

Auckland
Bangkok (Krung-Thep)
Beijing (Peking)
Christchurch
Darwin
Hanoi
Hobart
Ho Chi Minh (Saigon)
Hong Kong
Jakarta
Kuala Lumpur
Manila
Melbourne
Perth
Phnom Penh
Shanghai
Singapore
Soul (Seoul)
Sydney
Tokyo
Vladivostok
Wellington

SMALL ISLANDS ?

Aleutian Islands
Christmas Isles
Fiji
Kiribati (Gilbert Islands)
Kuril Islands
Hawaiian Isles
Marshall Isles
Midway
New Caledonia
Solomon Isles
Timor
Tuvalu (Ellice Islands)

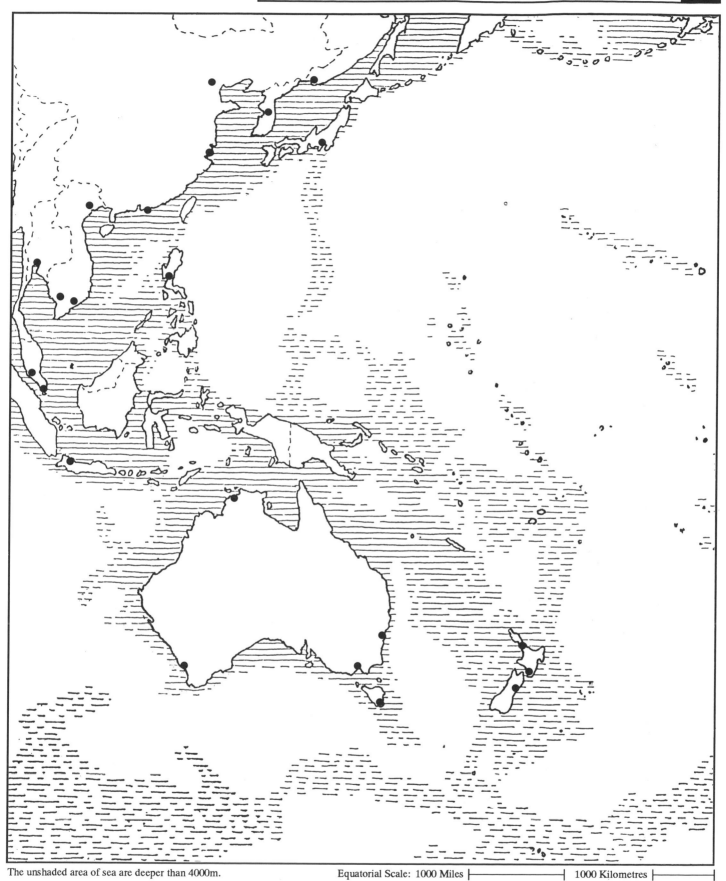

The unshaded area of sea are deeper than 4000m.

Equatorial Scale: 1000 Miles ├─────┤   1000 Kilometres ├─────┤

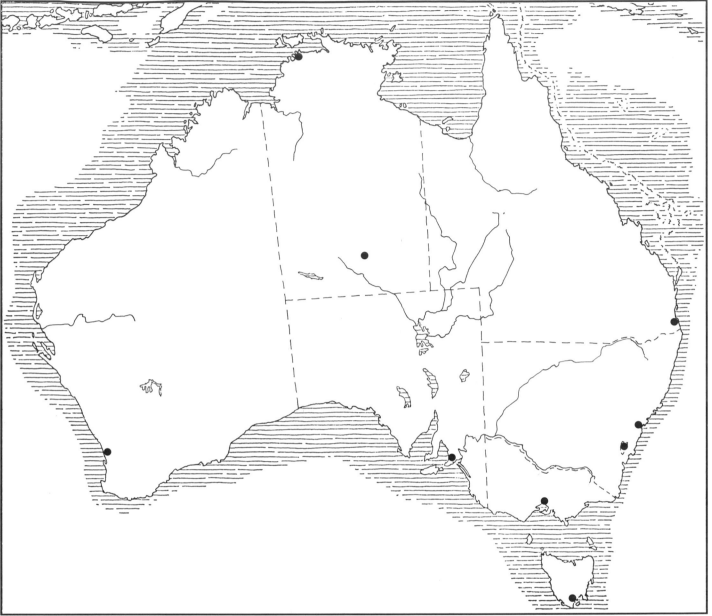

The unshaded areas of sea are deeper than 2000m.

500 Miles ├─────────────┤   500 Kilometres ├─────┤

? OCEANS & SEAS

Indian Ocean	Bass Str.
Pacific Ocean	Botany Bay
Arafura Sea	Great Australian Bight
Coral Sea	Gulf of Carpentaria
Tasman Sea	Joseph Bonaparte Gulf
Timor Sea	

? LAKES & RIVERS

Lake Amadeus	Cooper Creek	The Flinders
Lake Barlee	The Darling	The Gascoyne
Lake Eyre	The Diamantina	The Georgina
Lake Frome	The Finke	The Murray
Lake Gardner	The Fitzroy	The Victoria
Lake Torrens		

? STATES & CITIES

Australian Capital Territory	Adelaide
New South Wales	Alice Springs
Northern Territory	Brisbane
Queensland	Canberra
South Australia	Darwin
Tasmania	Hobart
Victoria	Melbourne
Western Australia	Perth
	Sydney

? MAJOR FEATURES

Great Barrier Reef
Great Dividing Range
Gibson Desert
Great Sandy Desert
Great Victoria Desert
Simpson Desert
Tanami Desert

NEW ZEALAND **?**

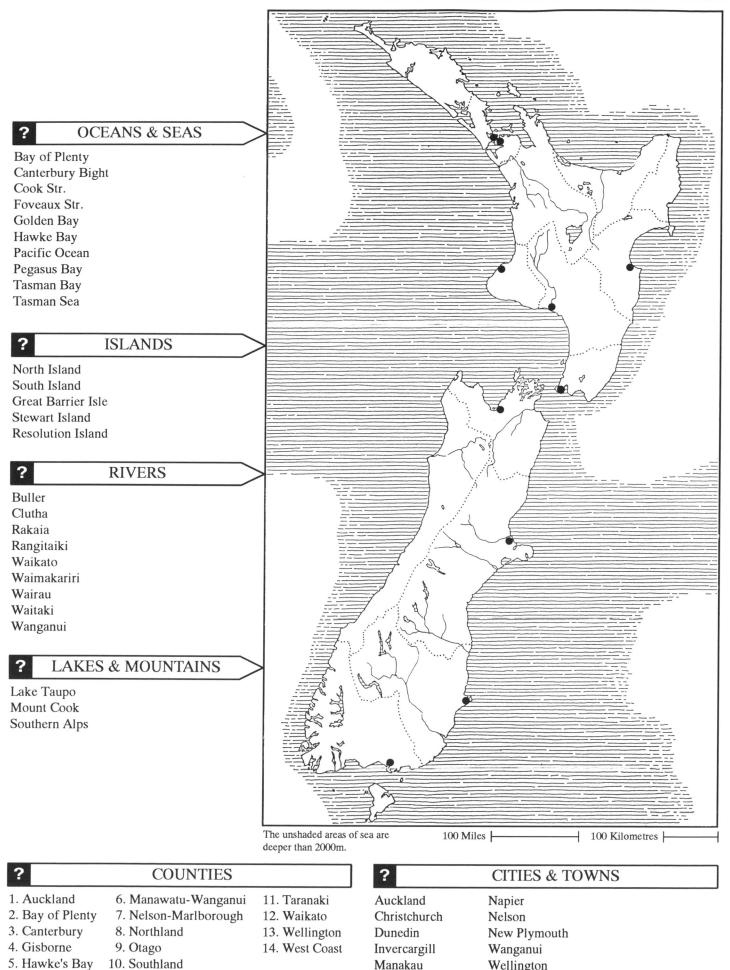

The unshaded areas of sea are deeper than 2000m.

100 Miles

100 Kilometres

Know Asia!

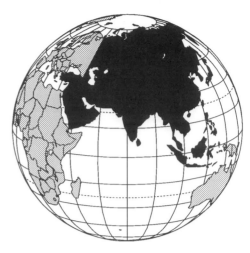

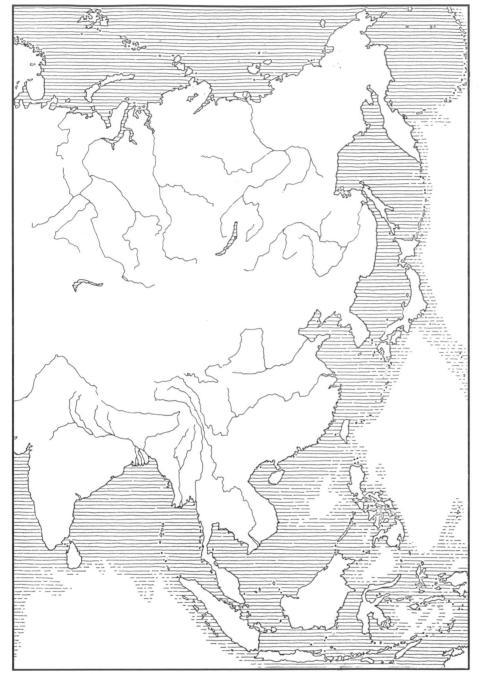

The unshaded areas of sea are deeper than 4000m.

— 24 —

? COUNTRIES

Afghanistan	Kyrgyzstan
Bangladesh	Laos
Bhutan	Malaysia
Brunei	Mongolia
Burma (Myanmar)	Nepal
Cambodia (Kampuchea)	Pakistan
China	Philippines
(Sinkiang)	Russian Federation
(Tibet)	Sri Lanka
India	Taiwan
Indonesia	Tajikistan
Iran	Thailand
Japan	Turkmenistan
Kazakhstan	Uzbekistan
North Korea	Vietnam
South Korea	

? SEAS & ISLANDS

Arctic Ocean	Andaman Islands
Indian Ocean	Borneo
Pacific Ocean	Hainan
Andaman Sea	Japan
Bering Sea	Java
East China Sea	Nicobar Islands
South China Sea	Philippines
Sea of Japan	Sri Lanka
Sea of Okhotsk	Sulawesi (Celebes)
Yellow Sea	Sumatra
Bay of Bengal	Taiwan
Gulf of Thailand	

? LAKES & RIVERS

Lake Baikal	The Pechora
Lake Balkhash	The Salween
The Amur	The Yenisey
The Brahmaputra	
The Chang Jiang (Yangtze)	
The Ganges	
The Huang He (Yellow)	
The Indus	
The Irrawady	
The Lena	
The Mekong	
The Ob'	

? MOUNTAINS & DESERTS

Central Siberian Plateau
Gobi Desert
Himalaya Mountains
Hindu Kush
Thar Desert
Tibetan Plateau
Ural Mountains
West Siberian Plain

1000 Miles ⊢——————⊣   1000 Kilometres ⊢——————⊣

? CITIES

Alma-Ata	Dushanbe	Jakarta	Manila	Tashkent
Bangkok (Krug-Thep)	Frunze	Kabul	Phnom Penh	Thimphu (Thimbu)
Beijing (Peking)	Guangzhou (Canton)	Karachi	Pyongyang	Tientsin
Bombay	Hanoi	Kathmandu	Samarkand	Tokyo
Calcutta	Harbin	Kuala Lumpur	Soul (Seoul)	Ulaanbaatar (Ulan Bator)
Colombo	Ho Chi Minh (Saigon)	Lhasa	Shanghai	Viangchan (Vientianne)
Dehli	Hong Kong	Madras	Singapore	Vladivostok
Dhaka (Dacca)	Irkutsk	Mandalay	T'ai-pei	Yangon (Rangoon)

Know the Middle East!

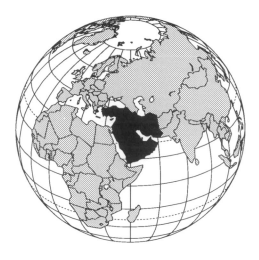

SEAS & RIVERS

Indian Ocean	The Amudar'ya
Arabian Sea	The Don
Aral Sea	The Euphrates
Sea of Azov	The Nile
Black Sea	The Tigris
Caspian Sea	The Volga
Dead Sea	
Mediterranean Sea	
Red Sea	
Gulf of Aden	
Gulf of Oman	
Persian Gulf	
Strait of Hormuz	
Suez Canal	

? CITIES

Adis Abeba (Addis Ababa)	Gaza
Aden	Istanbul
Amman	Jerusalem
Ankara	Khartoum
Ar Riyad (Riyad)	Kuwait
Astrakhan	Makkah (Mecca)
Baghdad	Masqat (Muscat)
Bahrain	Port Said
Baku	Rostov na-Dony
Basra	Tashkent
Beyrouth (Beirut)	Tbilisi
Cairo	Tehran
Haifa	Tel-Aviv
Dimashq (Damascus)	Yerevan
Dubai	

? COUNTRIES

Afghanistan	Iran
Armenia	Iraq
Azerbaijan	Israel
Cyprus	Jordan
Djibouti	Kazakhstan
Egypt	Kuwait
Ethiopia	Lebanon
Georgia	Oman

? REGIONS

Arabia
Asia Minor
Mesopotamia
Sinai
The Crimea
The Holy Land
The Levant

THE BLACK SEA & THE CASPIAN SEA

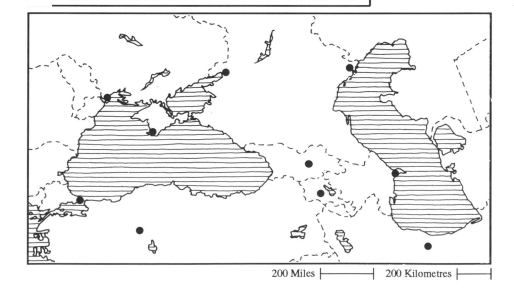

| 200 Miles ├──────┤ | 200 Kilometres ├──────┤ |

COUNTRIES

Armenia	Romania
Azerbaijan	Russian Federation
Bulgaria	Turkey
Georgia	Turkmenistan
Iran	Ukraine
Kazakhstan	Uzbekistan
Moldavia	

? CITIES

Ankara	Rostov na-Dony
Astrakhan	Sevastopol (Sebastopol)
Baku	Tbilisi
Istanbul	Teheran
Odessa	Yerevan

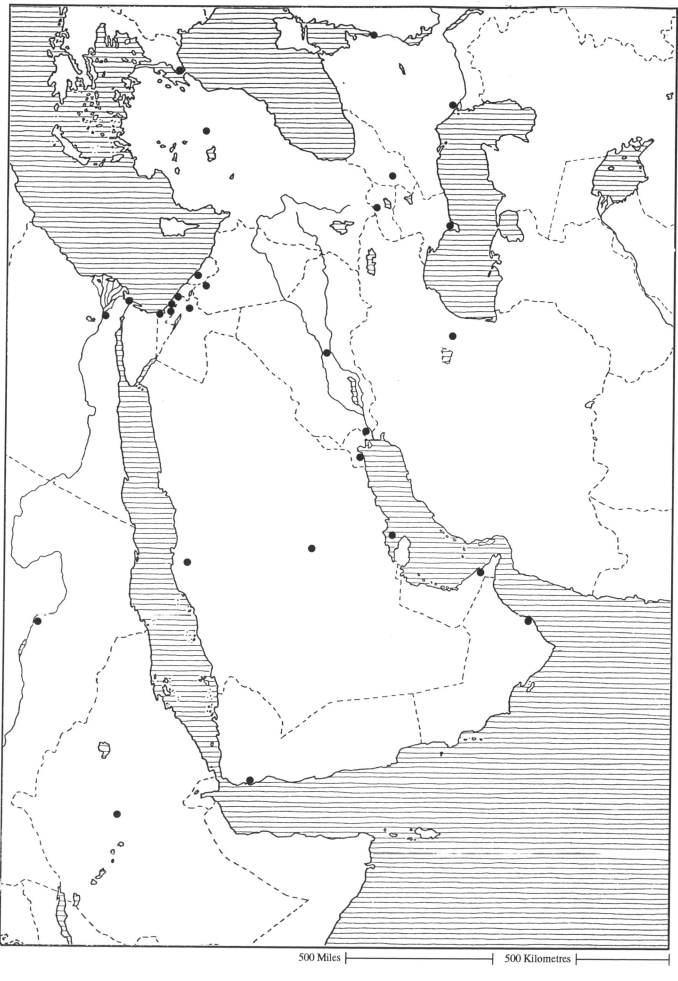

500 Miles

500 Kilometres

? INDIA

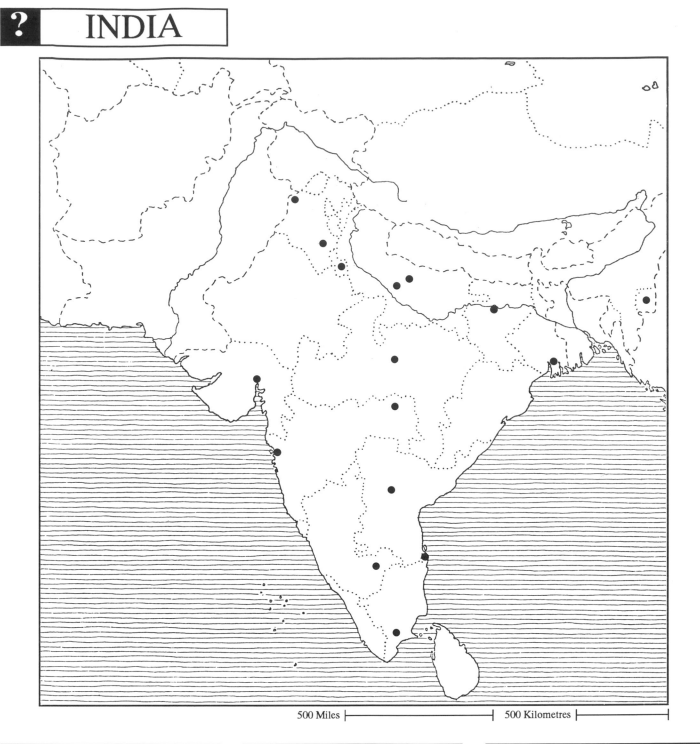

500 Miles | 500 Kilometres |

?	SEAS & ISLANDS
Indian Ocean	Lakshadweep Isles
Arabian Sea	Maldive Isles
Gulf of Manaar	Sri Lanka
Bay of Bengal	
Palk Strait	

?	MOUNTAINS & RIVERS
Deccan	The Brahmaputra
Western Ghats	The Ganges
Eastern Ghats	The Indus
Himalayas	
Hindu Kush	

?	COUNTRIES
India	China
Afghanistan	(Tibet) (Sinkiang)
Bangladesh	Nepal
Bhutan	Pakistan
Burma (Myanmar)	Sri Lanka

?	CITIES
Agra	Imphal
Ahmadabad	Jabalpur
Amritsar	Kanpur
Bangalore	Lucknow
Bombay	Madras
Calcutta	Madurai
Delhi	Nagpur
Hyderabad	Patna

?	STATES		
1. Andhra Pradesh	9. Kerala	17. Rajasthan
2. Assam	10. Madhya Pradesh	18. Sikkim
3. Bihar	11. Maharashtra	19. Tamil Nadu
4. Gujarat	12. Manipur	20. Tripura
5. Haryana	13. Meghalaya	21. Uttar Pradesh
6. Himachal Pradesh	14. Nagaland	22. West Bengal
7. Jammu & Kashmir	15. Orissa	
8. Karnataka	16. Punjab	

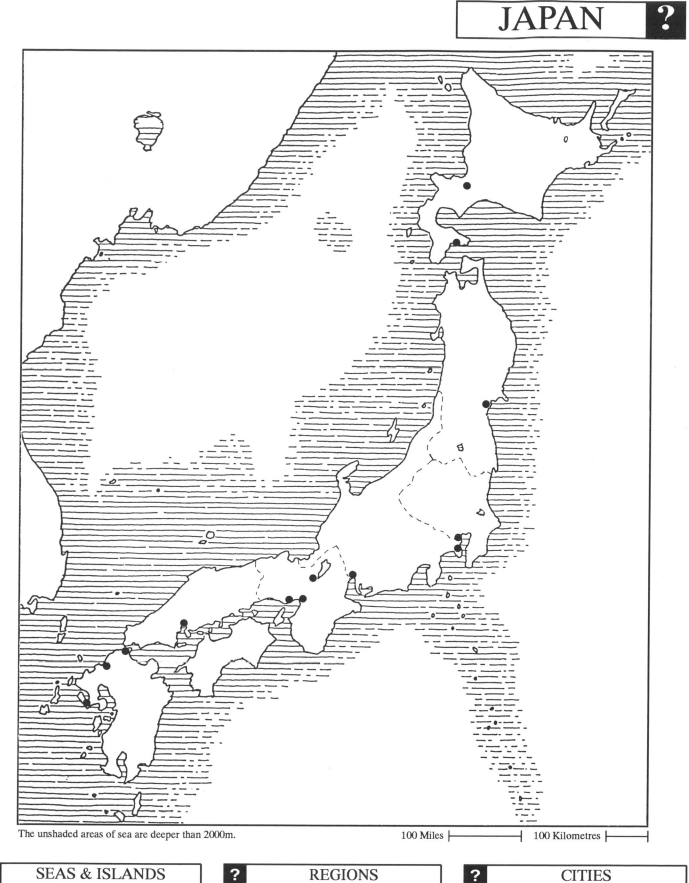

JAPAN ?

The unshaded areas of sea are deeper than 2000m.

100 Miles ├────────┤ 100 Kilometres ├────────┤

<table>
<tr><td>?</td><td colspan="2">SEAS & ISLANDS</td></tr>
</table>

Pacific Ocean	Hokkaido
East China Sea	Honshu
Sea of Japan	Kyushu
Korea Str.	Shikoku

<table>
<tr><td>?</td><td colspan="2">REGIONS</td></tr>
</table>

Chubu	Kyushu
Chugoku	Shikoku
Hokkaido	Tohoku
Kanto	
Kinki	

<table>
<tr><td>?</td><td colspan="2">CITIES</td></tr>
</table>

Fukuoka	Nagoya
Hakodate	Osaka
Hiroshima	Sapporo
Kita-Kyushu	Sendai
Kobe	Tokyo
Kyoto	Yokohama
Nagasaki	

? THE ATLANTIC

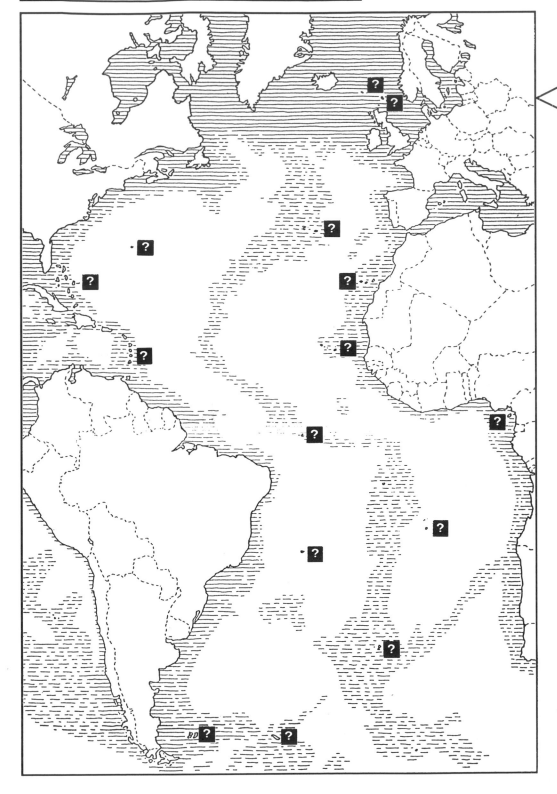

SMALL ISLANDS ?

Antilles
Ascension
Azores
Bahamas
Bermuda
Canaries
Cape Verde
Falklands (Malvinas)
Faroes
Fernando Po
Orkney & Shetland
St. Helena
St. Paul Rocks
South Georgia
Trinidad
Tristan da Cunha

? OCEANS & SEAS

North Atlantic Ocean	Baffin Bay
South Atlantic Ocean	Bay of Biscay
Baltic Sea	Hudson Bay
Caribbean Sea	Davis Str.
Mediterranean Sea	Denmark Str.
North Sea	Drake Passage
Norwegian Sea	Str. of Gibraltar
Sargasso Sea	Str. of Magellan
Scotia Sea	

? LARGE ISLANDS

Britain
Cuba
Greenland
Hispaniola
Iceland
Ireland
Jamaica
Newfoundland
Puerto Rico

? CAPES

Cape Farewell
Cape Finistere
Cape of Good Hope
Cape Horn
Cape Verde
John o' Groats
Land's End

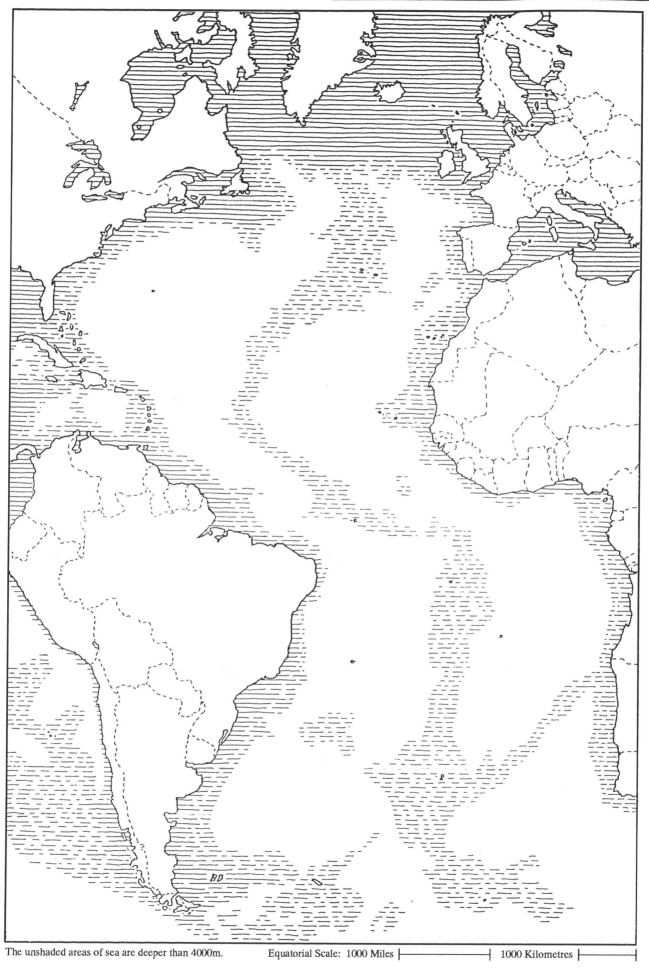

The unshaded areas of sea are deeper than 4000m.

Equatorial Scale: 1000 Miles ├────────┤   ├ 1000 Kilometres ├

Where is it!

1. The Pacific Ocean?
2. Cuba?
3. The Volga?
4. Burma?
5. Istanbul?
6. Uganda?
7. The Himalayas?
8. Auckland?
9. Moldavia?
10. Cape Horn?
11. Berlin?
12. Yemen?
13. Gibraltar?
14. The Danube?
15. Japan?
16. Tbilisi?
17. The Arabian Sea?
18. Jerusalem?
19. Brazil?
20. Sri Lanka?

Where is it!

1. Lake Baikal?
2. Romania?
3. The Thames?
4. India?
5. The Rockies?
6. Chicago?
7. Pakistan?
8. The Hindu Kush?
9. Vietnam?
10. The Persian Gulf?
11. Ireland?
12. The Gobi Desert?
13. Minsk?
14. Argentina?
15. Stockholm?
16. Queensland?
17. Zagreb?
18. Azerbaijan?
19. Israel?
20. Johannesburg?

Where are they!

1. The Alps?
2. Cape Horn and the Cape of Good Hope?
3. The Coral Seas?
4. Edinburgh and Dunedin?
5. The Bahamas?
6. Niger and Nigeria?
7. The Urals?
8. North Island and South Island?
9. The White Nile and the Blue Nile?
10. The Hebrides?
11. Niagara Falls?
12. The Himalayas?
13. The Kalahari and Sahara Deserts?
14. The Murray and the Darling?
15. Greenland and Iceland?
16. The Maldive Islands?
17. North and South Dakota?
18. The Falklands?
19. The Panama and Suez Canals?
20. The Appalachians?